Old Things

Ann Alexander

Ward Wood Publishing
www.wardwoodpublishing.co.uk

Published by Ward Wood Publishing
6 The Drive
Golders Green
London NW11 9SR
www.wardwoodpublishing.co.uk

The right of Ann Alexander to be identified as author of this work has been asserted by her in accordance with the Copyright, Designs and Patent Act, 1988.
Copyright © 2016 Ann Alexander
ISBN: 978-1-908742-55-1

British Library Cataloguing in Publication Data. A CIP record for this book can be obtained from the British Library.

All rights reserved. No part of this publication may be reproduced, stored in a retrieval system, or transmitted in any form or by any means, electronic, mechanical, photocopying, recording or otherwise without the prior written permission of the publishers. This book may not be lent, hired out, resold or otherwise disposed of by way of trade in any form of binding or cover other than that in which it is published, without the prior consent of the publishers.

Designed and typeset in Palatino Linotype by
Ward Wood Publishing.

Cover design by Ward Wood Publishing.
Artwork: Three dolls © Maarten Van Der Kroft
Supplied by agency: Dreamstime.com

Printed and bound in Great Britain by
Imprint Digital, Seychelles Farm,
Upton Pyne, Exeter, Devon EX5 5HY

For the loved and the lost

Contents

To the front as night is falling	11
The senior lecturer in astronomy drops her purse in Waitrose	12
The day they let the animals out	13
If present trends continue	14
How to knock fifty years off your age	15
Under the tree	16
On a scale of nought to ten	17
Dead cat poem	18
The small death of Bob	19
Lies, and damn lies	20
Where old languages go to die	21
North Atlantic in a storm	22
The Monday sea	23
Living next door to the sea	24
Condolences in the deli aisle at Tesco	25
Watching my mother turn into a wasp	26
Blue curtains	27
We are standing in front of something unimaginably large	28
The old soldiers in the chemo ward	29
Phone box sex	30
Woman in the landscape	31
I'm going to have to let it go	32
Old things	33
If only I knew where you were going	34
I know what love feels like	35
If you go back far enough	36
Ton-up and terrified	37
Train from Torbay to Newton Abbott	38

Wearing her baby	39
Power dressing	40
My father works with mercury	41
Song of the naked mole rat	42
Too far in the wrong shoes	43
When the end comes	44
Three women in a car	45
Gertrude Stein was right	46
Two subjects looking for a verb	47
End of	48
A sporting chance	49
Generally speaking	50
The magistrate	51
Foul squared	52
Speculation	53
Down the black hole	54
Let us live backwards now	55
The nocturnal habits of old men	56
Cursing the miracle	57
Putting out the prayer flags	58
Day trip to the Bishop Rock lighthouse	59
An Ad Man remembers the slogans of his youth	60
Doctored	61
The cruel trade in animal metaphors	62
The first time ever I	63
The loneliness of the long distance mother	64
Aslant	65
Dichotomy woman	66
The libation	67
Another local scandal	68
Dolly Parton is five days older than me	69
At Circular Quay	70
A-Z of things not to do in the street	71
Street theatre	72

The running of the bulls	73
MH17	74
Full circle	75
Aftermouth	76
The baby gardener	77
A teenage girl discusses the situation with her mother	78
The old order	79
Grade Two Listed	80
Tomorrow I will pull myself together	82
I did it for you	84
Acknowledgements	85

Old Things

To the front, as night is falling

Those who set up home by the sea
must consider the tides, and we do.

At the end of the day we walk to the sea, and talk
of the incoming, outgoing, neap and full,
high, ebb, spring and flood of the tides.

We consider the moon that sucks the tides;
full, horned, gibbous and pale,
waxing and waning, ringed and red.

The children, the ecstatic dogs,
louche youths under the granite walls,
have gone to earth.

Unobserved,
we sniff the wind that tickles the waves:
simoom, sirocco, willywar, breeze;
dip our squealing toes in the gravelly sea;

imagine the world that lies beneath –
its mountains and rifts, its wrecks, its bones;
the uplifting, collapsing of rock.

> Each morning he gets up,
> shakes his memory and the day to life –
> and if his eyes, his ears, his legs
> are every day a little less,
> the balance holds. Evening will come.

Walk me to the sea, he says then,
holding out his hand to save me from drowning.

The senior lecturer in astronomy drops her purse in Waitrose

Coins rolling, spinning round her feet
and she thinks
I do not belong here
I am out of my orbit.

Behind her in the queue
shoppers tsk and frown and think
uncharitable thoughts about old women.

She thinks of planets, galaxies, the universe
spinning ever outwards and away,
rolling under desks and out of reach and sight;

and suddenly an idea hits her like a meteor
as they walk her to a chair,
collect what coins they can
and return them to her purse;

and when they ask if there is something they can bring
she says yes, pen and paper please

but they don't seem to hear and say instead
here's your shopping darling
is there someone we can call?

The day they let the animals out

Years of debate, and at last a decision.

The Traditionalists declared
Carry on as before, a zoo is part of being British.

The Sentimentalists pleaded
Trust in the essential goodness of the animals.

The Bishops intoned
The lion will lie down with the lamb.

The Pessimists shrugged
We're all going to die anyway.

The Politicians squirmed
There are no votes in the monkey house.

The Pragmatists argued
We can't afford to run it. So we won't.

The Revolutionaries roared
Any kind of freedom is better than none.

The Developers calculated
4,000 executive homes and a shopping mall.

The Optimists carried the day,
as they had always known they would.
Everything, they said, *will be fine in the end.*

The daily commute was suddenly much more interesting.
But the old and wobbly stayed indoors,
enquired about lion-proof fencing,
in spite of being assured by the Optimists
that it was perfectly safe to go out.

If present trends continue

Scientists believe, predict, that if and should,
we'll all be – that's a proven fact.

Scientists assert (and to a man,
or possibly a woman) even if, or when,
or by some chance, Black Swan Event, a blip,
an unforeseen, a bolt from out of –
it *will* all be so. No doubt about it,

after 2050 it will *all* be, and if not
because it's now too late, too soon;
(and in a year or three or when
grandchildren have grown, or if or why),

the figures show, the graphs foretell,
the data proves, the maths add up,
the tests reveal, computer models demonstrate
beyond the shadow of a reasonable doubt,

a poem *will* be written, even though
(if present trends continue)
no-one will be left on earth to read it.

How to knock fifty years off your age

Visit your mother. Note the weather.
Read the map of her face. Hard going, today.
Parry with talk of the rain outside
and the pain inside.

What have you been up to?
her voice is lemons and sermons.

You give the edited version, leaving out
the sex and drugs and rock and roll.
You keep an eye on the door.

She purses her lips. *Help me up.*
You pull her to her feet.

You're a good girl, she says,
to my white hair.
You hand over the flowers. *Happy Mother's!*
you say, closing your eyes for the kiss
that never comes.

Under the tree

This is the present that nobody wanted.
This is the present in secondhand wrapper
we thought was intended for some other person.

Not big, but it's bulky. Perhaps it's a sweater,
some socks and a tie, or a book about cooking;
a game so outmoded that no-one will play it.

A cake past its sell-by date, blue with bacteria,
fake leopard scarf with embarrassing staining,
hideous clock, or shocking pink stockings

that glow in the dark. The present sits waiting.
This is the present that someone has planted
under the tree while we weren't even looking.

Now it's the middle of March, and it's raining,
the tree long dismantled, the baubles in tissue.
No name tag, no pack drill, the ribbon's gone missing.

The present is coming apart on the carpet
as if it's alive. Now we cannot postpone it.
We tremble, we finger it, open it, own it.

On a scale of nought to ten

Where ten equals *the depth and breadth and height*
and nought equals *why are you stalking me?*

Where nine equals *as long as we both shall live*
and one equals *I said no yesterday and I'm saying no today.*

And eight equals *fingers crossed, this one is different*
and two equals *it's not your fault, it's mine*

And seven equals *a dozen red roses, and "sorry" on the card*
and three equals *just don't take me for granted*

And six equals *I want to be with you all the time*
and four equals *we can't be together all the time*

And five equals *sometimes I do and sometimes I don't*
but stick around and it just might work –

how do you love me?

Dead cat poem

She who flowed like mercury, or mist
over silent fields,
who had seen off foxes,
terrorized hedgerows, endangered
several species of rodent,
was now sitting on death's lap
and feeling his cold fingers.

We stood and looked for signs of her
in the grey bundle we had petted and stroked,
lugged and loved through the years.
But she was looking elsewhere,
untidy for the first time,
dusty and in disarray.

Strange that when we buried her
beneath a flowering bush, in the sunny place
where she loved to sit,
we could not touch her.
Scooped her up with a spade.

The small death of Bob

Who saw him die?
>He lived a short, tight life, and died
>without much fuss or any company.

Who'll bear his weight?
>They sent the budget Daimler for him.
>First time in a car for twenty years.
>Four bearers carried him – this man
>who could not find a woman or a friend.

Who'll be the priest?
>The unknown vicar signed him off
>with forty-six crisp words.
>He got his dates of birth and death
>mixed up with those of Millicent,
>waiting with her mourners by the door.
>Officially, Bob grew younger after death.

Who'll sing a psalm?
>Afterwards, the six of us (plus dog)
>made chilly small talk in the Royal Oak,
>raised a glass, and murmured platitudes.
>Later still, a man sang Danny Boy
>but none of us joined in.

Who'll toll the bell?
>His distant cousin wondered as they left:
>did he own that house of his,
>or rent? What were the odds
>he'd get a little mention in his will?

Lies, and damn lies

On the census form I write:
British/female/married/child.
Pretty much the plain unvarnished truth –
but elsewhere I play games.

On one such impudence, I morphed into
a twenty-nine-year-old Icelandic man
called Magnus, reek of sulphur clinging to
my hand-knits, hair a glacial blonde.

Another time, my great great Grandma's
hot Italian blood (disputed) got a furious outing.
Age? *Nineteen*, I write, *but feeling thirty six*.

A form demands to know my married state.
I write *it's complicated*. It persists –
Straight/gay/bi/transgender/married/other?
I scribble *other* –
sometimes with a lengthy note attached.
Sex? They ask. *Just once*, I write, or
Chance would be a fine thing. Bring it on.

The point is to confuse, while simultaneously
undermining stereotypes. The kind of thing
a lady from New Guinea (thirty-two, no kids)
might do to pass the time. *Who'd have thought,*
they might be saying in Research,
that such a large and various troupe
of circus riders from Mongolia
was living in that cottage, in that little Cornish town?

Where old languages go to die

When no-one cares about them any more
when absolutely nobody cares –

when they can no longer ask for a loaf of bread
or remember the word for bread –

when there is no-one to talk to
even to say I love you –

and the world is forever inventing things
for which they have no name –

and no way to know the purpose of the thing
for which they have no name;

the old languages walk out into the night
(they always walk, and they always walk slowly)

take themselves to an ancient place with
an ancient name: a cromlech, a fogou, a carn

and wait there, for tens, for hundreds of years
till they fade to a shadow of a shade

under the stars, for which they have a name,
a different name, given when everyone thought
the stars would last for ever.

North Atlantic, in a storm

The word *waves* is too friendly for this sea,
bringing to mind a disembodied royal hand
acknowledging the crowd,
or the corrugated playground of a beach.
Adding *thirty foot* is not enough.

The word *sea* is too safe,
suggesting the Med or Red or the Dead,
or even the silent Sargasso.

I try *the ocean, the main, the deep, the high,
the trackless watery waste*
but these words are man-made, human sized.

This is no place for people,
or their regulated, so precise vocabulary –
what words are equal to the task
of bringing this ferocity to the page?
I dip my toe in Thunderous,
I paddle among Mountainous.
I splash about in Awesome.

Drowning in adjectives, I give up –
describe myself instead: ashamed and small,
as if I had just been introduced to God,
and couldn't think what to say.

The Monday sea

On Sunday, like an Old Testament prophet,
the sea roared warnings
over the rusty railings of the prom.

The old penitents crouched in the shelter,
heads down, tut-tutting over
the inky Sins of the World.

The owners of insistent dogs
genuflected in the wind
until the ritual of the plastic bags was done.

How blameless the sea looks,
under the Monday sky
even though the workaday beach
is littered with the memory of the storm.

Living next door to the sea

is like living next to a man
with an unpredictable temper and a pit bull.

You smile when you see it, say *good morning sea,*
squinting sideways for signs
of mood change, a darkening, an unusual quiet,
the absence of birds.

Some days it's ok to walk the beach,
gathering stones, or even dip the toes.
The sea lies flat in the sun, growling in its sleep.

Other times you're grateful for the garden fence,
the space between.

Then you wonder if the fence would make
the slightest difference, if push came to shove;

or the space between mean anything at all,
under a full moon, with a spring tide,
when a tremor far away shakes the earth
and sends that wet fist
towards your little certainties.

Condolences in the deli aisle at Tesco

Once you've passed the meals for one
and the buy-one-get-one-free bananas
there is no escape.

You will have to pay
for your trolley-dash to normal,
as a woman you hardly know
takes you by the arm and says *so sad to hear*.

She weighs your grief
and follows up with *such a lovely man*
as if you needed telling, and you look
desperately from left to right

but you are too far in and so you stare
hard at the herbal teas,
because for some reason it would be
the worst betrayal yet to cry here now

in front of her, this stranger,
in front of the freeze-dried lemon zest.

Watching my mother turn into a wasp

Tiny and yellow, suddenly furious –
she settles on the chair, clutches her bag,
and rages; but her voice is muffled, small,

as if under glass. We watch her
scrabbling to get at us, angry with the world.
Nobody nobody cares. She's terrified.

She will not eat. She says *oh let me die*
and then *I hate it here*. Whispers her rosary,
the first few words, droning from half-closed lips
HolymarymotherofGod, take me Jesus…
The eyes are small and black, unfocussed,
inward turned, seeing the terrible future,

the threatening shadows moving beyond reach.
She brushes off my hand. In her mind,
she hurls herself against unyielding glass,

to find a crack, a gap, a clean escape,
something, anything, half alive to sting.

Blue curtains

The small hours, and the blue light flashing
outside my window in the smartest hotel
in the smartest part of town

takes my mind to the plain room
above the cake shop,
two of us skinny on the brass bed,
thin blue curtains bellying
with the streetlight shining through,
the man-boy singing in my ear
here comes the sun.

We are standing in front of something unimaginably large

We move slowly as mime artists
pretending to climb stairs.
The light plays tricks with horizons.

What appears to be over there
is only a careless step away.
No colours interrupt the black, white and grey,
except the sun, setting like a blood orange.

We must decide: attempt the climb now,
or stay awhile at the inadequate hut
with nothing to comfort us
but blankets thrown across bare boards.
Going back is not an option.

Our phones have died.
We lost the maps miles ago.
In all likelihood only one of us will make it.

It's bloody cold and going to get colder.
The way back is blocked, and we are faced
with a long stay in the cold hut,

or tackling something unimaginably large –
wishing we had a map, or a phone,
or the slightest hope of ever getting back.

The old soldiers in the chemo ward

lie quiet, minds drifting off to childhood fields,
or else some long lost lover's bed.

They lie in rows, like soldiers at Rorke's Drift,
ignoring overwhelming odds, the far horizon.
Reality does not bear too much scrutiny.

In this lull they dream, the brave old boys.
Hope is a scarce commodity. Letting the side down
not an option here. Machines click, whirr.
Automatic answer: *Ticking over. Feeling fine.*

Attendants (answering to the name of wife)
murmur reassurance and are pretty much ignored.
They unpack rations, fiddle with the crossword,
settle for the long wait.

The heat is overwhelming, but the old men
shroud themselves in blankets, coats and scarves,
blend to the mottled space, observe the drip,
the dial, the seconds clicking by.

Eventually, they sleep.
Their sniper's eyes – only halfway closed –
snap wide with every movement by the door.
A nurse checks names and dates of birth,
as if some undeserving other would attempt
to intercept the weapons she will send into the heart.

Backs to the wall, facing out into a world
that clicks and whirrs and drips, the old men
do as they are told, perhaps for the first time.

Make a fist, my darling.
Aim, fire, here it comes.

Phone box sex

He leaves his BlackBerry at home.
No texts, no trace.
The rude red phone box calls.

Each night – *just popping out* –
his heart so loud it's giving him away.
dog needs walking…milk needs buying…
need a loaf… I need, need –

Phone at six, she said;
it's four o'clock, it's five, it's five oh eight oh, oh,
oh please *be* there, dear disembodied voice
in my red Tardis, stiff with secrets,
aching for my call.

Beyond the sight of house and home
and wife, he runs with the dog
to his most happy place, endures
the smell, the guilt, the claustrophobia;
gasping for her voice, her promises, her love.

    Sometimes his wife says:
    wait a sec, I'll come along.

And then the wasted night.
They walk the dog. They go the other way.
They buy the milk. They choose a loaf.

While in another part of town,
the rude red phone box waits, its door ajar;
stiff with secrets, aching for his voice.

Woman in the landscape

Around the summit, clouds threaten rain.
It was beautiful yesterday, in the city park.

Someone's cousin had a great idea –
leave the dirty city, breathe some fresh clean air.
I went along with it, I always go along.

I do not know the name of this place,
or the village far below.
I know we drove, days, nights;
ten of us inside the bus.

Later, we walked upwards, over stones;
past unfriendly faces, almost naked women,
men muttering.

Yet that summit's still so far away.
I remember – *Dhuhr.* I turn my face,
pray *no more climbing, please.*

Close my eyes. Remember the baked village.
That other, distant, mountain
no-one would have wanted me to climb.

Open them on green.
This is not my own idea of beauty.
Like a whip, this *fresh clean air.*

My uncle spreads his arms.
The wind billows my burqa,
blue as that remembered sky.

Perhaps I will float upwards, out of here.
Family anchor me: sisters, cousins.
I turn my face. I close my eyes. Give thanks.

I'm going to have to let it go

said my friend the Scientist,
cradling the wounded bird.

Yes, I thought, set it free
to mend itself in the wood, to be itself.
Get your great hands off its softness,
allow the tiny heart to slow its pace,
let fear leave the brilliant eyes
and stop thinking yourself God.

But I had misunderstood,
for he was walking away from me,
and when I saw him lay the sparrow down
it did not move again.

Not suffering now, he said,
looking about for something else to cure.

Old things

Always loved old things – houses, chairs, art;
their cracks and stains, their history;
never tire of their foxed beauty.

People, too: Grandpa, crazed
in his creaking chair, torching a rollup;
corseted Granny, and above all, you.
Fragile you, an old lion
thorn-footed on the unforgiving plain,
bowing your head to the weather.

Always loved old things.
The way they don't quite work.
The way drawers stick, and insects set up home
in fantail joints; the inky evidence
of other people's ownership, the way
stuffing sprouts in tufts
through the bald brocade, the way they sag,
yet still look right in their established place,
telling their well-worn tales.

If only I knew where you were going

the language, the customs,
the weight you must carry on your soul's back.

Which direction? Who will be waiting?
Will anyone at all be waiting? If only I knew,
why, then I might – if only I knew

how warm the welcome would be,
whether the going would hit you hard or soft,
how you intend to explain yourself
when you are there. There are those

who swear they know, promise you this and that.
You half believe, but still you stay,
reluctant to start. The time will come

when we two will be forced to say goodbye.
But how will I get in touch?
Will I, won't I, see you again?

Even before you've gone I'm missing you,
even before you've gone
I'm crying wish you, wish you were here.

I know what love feels like

My ancient mother, in confession mode,
announces this:
    He loved you, in his way.
I'm silent on the phone, remembering.
    Men acted different, then.
I let it pass. And yet I want to tell her how
my life has been so blessed. I want to say
It's ok, Mum.
I know the way it feels to love, be loved.
    They didn't show their feelings
    like they do today.
Ah, no, how easy though for him to show
his anger at the world.

I'm silent still, remembering
the things I'm anxious to forget. I want to say:
It's ok, Mum. It didn't matter much.
I know what love feels like, I am beloved.
I have been blessed.

If you go back far enough

past the hand-me-down hardness
of dead generations, misplaced children,
dirt-encrusted men who begat
the skinny forebears who begat
your father's mother's father;
beyond the barely registered foot soldiers,
the hanged, the hungry, the anonymous,
the come-by-chance, the fly-by-nights,
the best-left-alone leaves on the family tree;
somewhere beyond the tinkling teacups,
the first-born, first-died, names
hanging on the old barbed wire,
the itinerant, the tarts, the tinners;
through the woebegone centuries
of soft men and hard women
tumble-weeding back through time
this way, sideways, half schooled or not at all,
blamed and blameless, caught in every storm,
minds shaped by canes and caveats;
go back far enough and you will find
the moment when
someone looked to the rising sun and thought:
What's over there? What is behind, beyond?
What if I leave all this,
right now,
and take the first step out, alone?

Ton-up and terrified

Each night at the school gate,
the man-boy, straddling
the muscle-bound mud-crusted monster
(called something like Viking or Vicious, or Thor)
idled his engine, for me.

I swung up behind, sixteen, and a handful,
helmetless, blazered, cheek on his leather back,
arms round his leather waist
straight to the highway the fast way
seventy eighty ninety a hundred
and no one at all approving.

And after, the layby,
throbbing, lubricious; leaning against
the bike's restless puttering
(Viper or Panther or Thunder or Storm),
kissing the boy, and both of us shaking
blood racing, eyes streaming
and all for a laugh, and all for a dare –

back on the bike again
seventy, eighty, ton-up and trembling,
kissing goodbye at the end of the yellowbrick
(time for the Homework and Telly and Tea)
back to the grey room
back to the grey food
and no one at all enquiring.

How did we *not* die?
How could they not know,
not smell the heat on me
(Castrol and Petrol and Leather and Sweat)
notice the red eyes, remark on the smirk,
the halo of wind-shocked hair?

Train from Torbay to Newton Abbott

All eyes measure him. I draw the short straw.
He throttles the pole beside my seat,
his tattoos an aide memoir:
I am a warrior. I was loved once.

He wears the story of his life on neck, on arms –
all the parts you see bear testament.
The hair is Genghis. Shaved, a pony tail on top
to lift him up to God.

Our eyes meet. I am in Sunday Best
but we, roughly the same age,
must tolerate each other on this country ride.

The thick coat smells of sleeping rough,
when coat becomes a pillow for the head,
all clothes worn, for fear of theft or cold.

He asks, politely: is it ok if I sit alongside you?
And then for seven miles
I wear his breath, as he explains
where he's going now, and where he's been.

Wearing her baby

Every morning she avoids the mirror,
wears what she wore the day before.
Then she puts her baby on.

Each day she puts her baby on.
He clings. She is the scuffed protector
of his small perfection.
He bawls, he mews. She's mute.

Never before so many glances,
never so much admired –
though not for her, she is invisible.

Women cluster round the sling. *So cute!*
His little coat, the lovely cap –
His fingers pinch her breast.
And look at the tiny boots!

Last night,
he threw up twice into her lap.

She reads the route map of the day
on teeshirt, jeans, her vast
front-fastening bra.
She puts her baby on. Each day
she steps, invisible, into the world.

Power dressing

It was not until he took off the English suit, the soft
    linen shirt,
the winged collar, the spotted tie with the elaborate knot,
    the spats,
the silver topped cane, the waistcoat, the gold fob watch
    and the silk hat

and put on
the dhoti
made from
khadi cloth;
white, coarse,
spun on a wheel
and woven
on the village loom,

that
he
put on
the power
to shake
an Empire
by the
scruff.

For Ghandi

My father works with mercury

At a safe distance from his hand
I watch the mercury roll across the bench,
pooling then splitting, then pooling again;
gathering nothing, rejecting the dust.

I put out a finger to touch.
The mercury races away from me,
scattering and pooling, silver beads
elusive among the shavings in the dust.

I put out a finger, try to touch.
He looks at me, lips pressed into a line.

It will not be touched.
Instead, I smell the brimstone
of the soldering iron;
see the vice clamped to the bench,
consider the sharp tools lined up in the black box;
see his initials burnt into everything,
everything but the mercury
scattering and pooling, over the dust.

Song of the naked mole rat

Punk rat, I am. You think
your ordinary rat is tough?
You've no idea.

OK, I'm pink enough. And yes,
I'm female, but don't think I'm nice.
I'm wrinkled, bald and blind.
So what, I have no hair?
Mess with me, I'll smell you out and bite –

these yellow teeth of mine
will rip the ground
from underneath your feet. Can't bear
the daylight world. The boiling sun
is not my friend. I make my life
here in my hole, halfway to hell,
breathing the grave's stale air.

Sex? More like a fight. *He's* half my size
and runs up from behind,
straddles my wrinkled arse.
All over in a shake. I'd kill him straight
but can't turn round.
He's off the way he came,
as fast reversing as in forward gear.

I'm no rat's wife. I'm queen
of this pink, squirming tribe
and I alone can mate.
I got the sticky end. But motherly, I ain't.
I'm Jenny Rotten rat. I'll still
be here when all you pretty creatures
meet your end.
Respect, my hairy friend.

Too far in the wrong shoes

We put them on for dancing
but now we find

our steps stumbling.
We have gone too far
to turn back now.

They are out of fashion,
they are suddenly too tight.

When the end comes

>You will be minding your own
in the garden, listening to a blackbird
astonishing an apple tree.
>>The end will unfold slowly, like a letter
in an unknown hand.

Or, in the middle of a dream of angels,
>as if out of nowhere the end will come –
pitiless, a buzzard on a lamb.

Perhaps you will be sprawled across
your lover's big brass bed,
while he shows you the colours of your mind –
>the end is a secret mischief, a clue written in blood.

In the company of hundreds, will you fall from the sky?
Will you walk in the wood, believing you are alone?
>The end will carry you away like a seventh wave.

Will you be moving towards the light,
down a tunnel that has no end?
Knifed by a stranger, for your mobile phone?
>Oh, the end will make you famous.

You will have your time on the stony hill,
however soft the journey to that place;
you will have that brief moment
you have rehearsed so long,
when you hang between two worlds
like a woman waking.

Three women in a car

We have no idea where we're going,
                except that it's
somewhere vaguely south
                          and it's threatening snow.

The car is old. Of course it's old;
          otherwise we could not have bought it.
None of us has ever
                    looked under the bonnet.

We are not running away, but running to.
                The possibility
of the car breaking down, is part
                          of the excitement.

The glory of the plan is
         there is no plan.
                    The uncertainty of the road,
      the unreliability of the car
sustain us.

All we know is, we are over love and under the influence.
          Uncertainty, unreliability ride in this car,
                travelling at speed
somewhere dangerously south.

Gertrude Stein was right

Those caught short of a quid in the Co-op, know;
the nodders and gophers, morning crush commuters –
all of them know it's better to be rich.

The numberless hordes in the lotto shop,
the scratchers, the beggars, the dole money divas,
they know – it's so much better to be rich

and turn your back on the stony ground;
move from the crummy block to the top address,
slide through the city in a big black car
in the finer than average dress.

And city boys, gambling their youth
on a cent here, a percentage there, they know
it's so much better to be rich.

The scholarship child at the famous school,
he knows, turning his cheek
from the sticks and stones.

The cold and sick, they know it too –
when the frail bones fail it's better by far
to jump the stumbling queue, straight to the man
with the top degree and the sure cure;

to skip the winter, raise a glass
of something as old as your grandpa, smell
a thousand different roses, roses,
everywhere, everywhere, all around.

Gertrude Stein:
I've been rich and I've been poor. It's better to be rich.

Two subjects looking for a verb

When we had all done flirting, dating,
moving on, moving in, promising,
sometimes quarrelling –

one active, the other passive;
one possessive, the other imperative –

and were suddenly aware we were moving
to that happy moment
when both agree (without speaking)
that this is definitely indicative.

Or, when one takes the hand of the other
without the other noticing
in the way a cat is suddenly present
all clause and purrs on your lap;

or you catch his eye over the heads of friends
and (without even speaking)
understand it's the time for conjugating –

then you are no longer you and I, but us
and you might as well, damn it all,
think about marrying.

End of

You stare blank-eyed at the future, and shake.
Gone without warning. His love,
the dream you have mortgaged your life on, has gone.

Substitutes offer relief, and you hit them hard.
You're crying from midnight to morning,
so thin you could break. You live on the phone.

You find yourself praying. You're pitiful,
shameless and shameful. You ache to the bone.

You lie on your bed. You lie to your friends.
Food sticks in your throat. Words stick in your throat.
You are flirting with death. You are socially dead.

And when you come out of it, after the numberless days,
there's a numbness of heart, a damage that clouds
your wept out eyes as you lie on the unmade bed.

Alone, through the cold turkey day after day of it.
Alone, through the wide-eyed foetal night of it.
Voices singing one song in your spaced-out head –

Got to get over this. Got to get through.
Got to get over him. Got to get through.

A sporting chance

He came first.
He celebrated, and the world
celebrated with him.
Next time, he came second.

The world talked about his premature decline,
and the sad ruin of a dream.
In order to come first again, he took a pill.

He took a pill each day. He stuck a needle in his arm.
He took a pill each day. He stuck a needle in his arm.

He came first. He sold his name.
The world celebrated with him.
He sold his soul and all his time.
He took a pill, he stuck a needle in his arm.

Someone saw him stick a needle in his arm.

He lost his deal.
Lost his wife. He lost his kids.
He lost his way. He lost his coach.
He lost his case. He lost his form.
He lost the race.

He took a pill. He stuck a needle in his arm.

Generally speaking

Men, it is said, love the idea of war,
especially when it is played on a computer
or from the safety of an armchair.
Women, it is said, love the idea of soldiers.

Men love pretending to be soldiers
but don't much like actually *being* soldiers
(unless they can be Generals).
Men generally like marching.

Women like watching men marching,
specially while wearing the kilt.
Women love soldiers but don't like the way
soldiers behave, unless they are marching.

Men like shouting and shooting at things,
but don't like being shouted at
by Sergeant Majors, or their wives,
or shot at by the enemy, even if they are
only playing a computer game.

Women don't like men being hurt
unless they are the ones doing the hurting.
Men love getting muddy
but don't like cleaning muddy boots.

Women love officers, especially in uniform,
but don't like clearing up the Officers' Mess.
Or mess in general, or even a General's mess.

Men like the company of women
but can't wait to get back to the company of soldiers,
before, during and after war,
especially if they are on the same side
and that side is winning.

The magistrate

After lunch, the magistrate was nicely in his stride –
Martini, claret, brandy, sloshed around his round inside.
His purple face was wet with sweat, his bloodshot eyes
    were bright
as he thought with yeasty pleasure of the feast to come
    that night.

The drunkard from the local park was brought up from
    the cells
and stood before the magistrate, with his attendant smells
that had their roots in good old Boots, or even B&Q
and came without a fancy name – in fact, were coloured
    blue.

The magistrate was merciless. *The folk who pay their rates*
don't want to see your boozer's face inside their new park gates.
It's not the first time you've stood here. Off you go below.
A week inside will show you there's a better way to go.

At four o'clock, the magistrate is stumbling to his car,
another day of justice done. He revs the Jaguar
and slopes off back to Solihull, to where he hopes to find
in a double gin and tonic, that elusive peace of mind.

Foul squared

In the coach, fifteen Olympians
descend upon this scuffed and rugged place.
Here for a rapid slaughter of the lambs,
the elbow in the groin, the boot in face.
And on the field, our team are set to lose.
The game begins to slip from bad to worse.
They might have struggled on. Instead they choose
the same sly kicks, the cuffs, the muttered curse.
And in the shower afterwards, the smell
of sweat and vinegar, and dirty feet,
and underpants. And something rank and fell
like long dead fish or stink of rotten meat.

Down the drain they shed the blood and sludge
and take into the world a hard won grudge.

Speculation

Suppose, in the sudden rush of our death,
hurtling from this world into the black,
you find yourself losing, then gasping for breath,
no sooner dead, than struggling back
red and bloody and full of alarm,
as another you, different, opens your eyes
to a strange breast, another dawn –
would this account for the look of surprise
on the face of the outraged newly born?

Down the black hole

She fell
hook line and sinking
past the jokes and the warning signs

down past the stiff upper lip
and into the rocky black
via the hard place

and it hurt.
Though there was
barely a mark on her
and nothing was broken
she couldn't, wouldn't move.

The faces and voices seemed so far away
they could not reach her.

Someone dropped a platitude
and left, shaking his head.
No-one down there, he said.

She howled
with her mouth wide open
but no words came,
down there,
where nothing grows but sad ferns,
straining for the light.

Not a trace of her was ever found,
although
someone leaner, lighter,
did eventually scramble out.

Let us live backwards now

Let your old bones unbend,
skin thicken and clear,
legs regain their strength, arms encircle.
Let lips meet, heart beat, blood race,
like a young man's heart;
let words be words of love
and not despair.
Let joy meet us and let our lives
lie before us like a book unread.

The days turn into weeks then years,
and love grows tired
and struggles underneath the weight
of age and medicines,
and hope that never goes
and always something new to try.

Nurses search for veins
in the old arm, touch the skin
as if it were a fine silk scarf,
and compliment this scholar
on remembering his date of birth;
and it is just as well

that when love came, a life ago,
it came with force enough
to lift me through this time,
for it is love that carries us
and love that makes you beautiful to me.

The nocturnal habits of old men

Old men leave their beds at night
as slyly as adulterers,
once, twice – their body clocks
chiming the wrong time.

Slipperless, they navigate
the landing to the loo
in the precarious dark.
Then, wide eyed at four,
grapple with old wives tales, old wives.
All through the incomprehensible day,
the old men keep their heads down,
sleep easy and loud,
long for the embrace of pyjamas,
go to bed at nine.
At night, though, they take their sleep
shallow and small; nap, groan, rise,
creak and shuffle round the house,
hands groping in the dark
for known landmarks, chairs, the table's edge.

Old men, on summer nights,
might dream of setting foot outside
with foxes, owls, and foraging cats,
but aren't allowed.
Instead their minds – unattached to now –
rise to meet imaginary paths,
pounce on a fleeting memory; or
hungry for air and space, open
wide their bedroom windows,
navigate the stars and think of God,
stare at the rising sun through misty eyes
and, like the owl, look down upon the world
grateful for one more day.

Cursing the miracle

This is about the (whisper it) time of the month
when nature nudges the life of a woman – or not.

And everywhere women and girls wake up
to the cramping knowledge of cycles and shifts,
the absence or presence of luck, as life
takes a turn for the better or worse;
check diaries, the moon, the ticks on the calendar,
lie, leap for joy, maybe talk to abortionists, angels,

or not. All over the world, women and girls
face a life that's budding (or not), in a mud hut,
a shanty town, tenement, tent, Park Avenue block,
or small back room; for the first time, the last time,
or never at all, with a cloudy heart or with joy;
reach for cloths, clouts, moss – swear,
praise the Lord, or rail at a masculine God.

Everywhere, women and girls
smile, groan, set off on the aching walk to the well,
the ride on the train; curl up in a downy bed
or the floor of a yurt, think of doctors, their priest,
the wise woman, witch, their mother, or no one at all;

As the chalice within us fills, flips, empties and fills,
and we are a pot, a pod, a pan, a grail,
an amphora, urn, a gourd; unclean, unloved, set aside;
the cherished, the treasure, the curse.

Putting out the prayer flags

Can't pray any more, and so
I let the wind do the praying for me.

I have done with asking God
for favours I have not earned,
promising to be good hereafter.
God will listen to the wind.

I don't expect the wind to ask for miracles,
only an easy passage for you,
my old ship
creaking out of harbour.

And the flags:
yellow, green, purple, red,
like a sailor's pennant:
England expects every man.
Farewell, welcome home.

Day trip to the Bishop Rock lighthouse

All quiet in St Mary's Pool, but I should have known
from the look on the boatman's face
that breakfast was a bad idea.

Bucking and rolling now, like a ride at the fair.
Then seriously wild. I grabbed the side of the boat,
held fast, leant out for an hour of terror, shame, regret

and astonishment. *Look,* someone said,
and I raised my white face from the sea,
looked up at the granite tower on a rock ledge, filling
    the sky

and was off again at the thought of it:
men so desperate for work
they'd tough it out for years to build this phallic gesture

to the rollercoasting sea which, today,
the boatman had described as *relatively calm.*
No-one died in the making,

although a century ago a ship
smacked right into it, six men lost in daylight.
When the sea was *relatively calm.*

An Ad Man remembers the slogans of his youth

Happiness comes in many shapes –
egg, cigar, warm gun.
But it's seldom old-shaped.

Old is the opposite of springtime fresh.
Old is the part nobody wants to reach,
where all slogans end.

In my green prime
I had the body of a much younger man,
the ring of confidence;
only my hairdresser knew for sure.

I was the one with the top job and the boss's ear –
the right one, the real thing, new, free, magic;
whiter than white, cool as a mountain stream,
a thousand-a-year man, with a neat wife
and a pert girl on my knee.

Tick followed tock,
and I found myself end-of-season,
so last-year, surplus to requirements,
a nine stone weakling, a drug on the market.

Comical as old technology, I am on my back,
gaping like a fish past its sell-by date,
a worn out fridge at the dump.

Your future may be orange:
mine is black. Everything must go.
I will shortly be remaindered, repackaged,
sold off cheap, on the back burner,
slung in a skip, buried and forgotten,
in the landfill site of dreams.

Doctored

Running like a new car he says
and reaches out a shaky hand, grins.
He has lived life at full throttle,
an editorial of benign denials.
They will come back, he says,
the good old days.

He told me, once: *In the war,*
they doctored the truth.
No-one wanted the bald facts.
That's how we won, darling.

We'll beat this, you'll see.
We ponder truth,
while a nurse
who isn't quite a nurse brings
a kind of tea.

The truth, that state of mind
he says there's no such thing as,
can still be glimpsed in the doctor's eyes,
or even, sometimes, in his own.

The cruel trade in animal metaphors

I speak on behalf of the fatted calf,
the snake in the grass, the toad in the hole,
the stubborn mule, the poor blind mole,
the running dog, the cruel cat,
the dirty pig, adulterous rat,
the busy bee, the vampire bat,
the tiger burning in the night,
the fish in the sea there's plenty more of,
the silly goose you can never be sure of,
the lion with his unfair share,
the antic-frantic mad March hare,
the randy rabbit, cooing dove,
weighed down with peace and hope, and love.
Who'd be the weeping crocodile,
the headless chicken, dying swan,
the silly, social butterfly,
the drunken newt, the blue-arsed fly,
the barrow-load of monkeys one
can never be more clever than?

Do animals think, as they sit in the sun
and ponder us humans, so very diverse,
how on the whole pleasant and friendly is man!
Or are we a meta for everything worse?

The first time ever I

Out of the fog of gas and air
my body crashed to earth,
while all attention moved

elsewhere.

My eyes closed, opened on your face.
My tiny moon. I read the map of you
as time began its long, slow fall,
smoothing you into

separateness.

The milky curiosity of your eyes
explored the blue of mine,
which had seen so much
and understood nothing

till this time.

Here is the Sea of Tranquillity.
There you are, lit from within,
the world's best gift to me,
quite undeserved.

Into my heart you crept,
and we began the long lesson of love.

The loneliness of the long distance mother

When time was small,
and the world the size and shape of a breast,
I could hear you breathe
through four walls,
could cover the ground between
faster than a flooding tide.

The worst sound of all
was the sound of you crying a long way off;
when I was the only one
who could stop the tears, singing out as I ran
hush babe, don't cry, I'm coming, I'm here.

Twenty years on you had to leave
to stretch the world,
spooling the thread between us over continents
as you invented names for me
that didn't mean *I need you*.
Our role reversal stings,
as sharp as paper bleeding a finger.

I am too old for new tricks now.
I am as fearful as a mouse
in a houseful of cats.

What sustains me?
The umbilical telephone cord.
What hurts me?
The emptiness in my stomach when you don't call;
the absence of your presence.
My sudden tears
at the sound of your voice a long way off,
saying *hush now Ma, don't cry, I'm here.*

Aslant

He came at a road diagonally,
    crossing as far from safe as he could get
        as if reluctant to leave danger behind,
            and bow down to cautious age.

He came at an argument that way, too,
    and he had plenty of them,
        searching for truth and beauty
            by the oddest routes.

We found him diagonal on the big bed,
    in the act of getting up;
        as if, while he was cross

and crosswise, an angel had called by
    and held out a hand to him
        saying, come on, no arguing now,

time for straight answers, time to leave.

Dichotomy Woman

She respects Aristotle, she argues for Kant,
will sit for hours and debate
whether there can or cannot be free will;
and she also believes in angels.

She dismisses socialism, materialism,
fascism, utilitarianism.
Questions the prejudice of history.
But she does believe in angels.

She knows their names:
Gabriel, Uriel, Lucifer, Wormwood.
She knows the work they do,
whether it's to guard the throne of God
or sing His praises for all eternity.

    Sometimes she loves him.
    Sometimes she hates him.
    Sometimes she is completely indifferent.
    Sometimes she doubts
    the very existence of love.

She reads her horoscope every day.
Other times, she argues with Aristotle;
and she sometimes believes in angels.

The libation

We flew back
to the bird encrusted island
we left you on, smuggling in
a damn fine Chateau-bottled red.

This is our Day of the Dead.
This rock your pyramid, and us
still needing you. We couldn't give you
terracotta soldiers, but we knew
what you'd ask for, if you could.

So we fought with gulls and a Force 8,
pulled the cork on our grief.
A glass apiece for us and one for you.
Threw words and wine into the wind.

The rock, shining after rain,
accepted the offering
your old fist
would happily have closed around.

A year since you became
one with the sea thrift.
Yet I swear your spirit lives on here.
Old men, old habits, die hard.

No better place to spend eternity.
You, bruised soul, as much a part of it
as rocks, wind, birds, the tears,
and now the good red wine.

Another local scandal

> All quiet on my blameless road,
> but turn the hectic page and see

killer dogs. A hopeless debt.
Something gross on the internet. An old man
murdered for his watch. A naked breast,
a woman mugged. A blind date
with a psychowitch. A bishop, utterly depraved.
A man enslaved. A slut no better than she ought.
Local big-wig, on the skids. A ponzi scheme.
Something vile to do with kids. A vicious war.

There's money involved, there always is.
And sex. And drugs. And dodgy Scotch
(from somewhere foreign, you can bet).
Sticky fingers in the till. A forged will.
A choirboy, led up the garden path.
A body lying in the bath. A broken dream.
The mayor, caught with his trousers down.
A sailboat, lured to a rocky shore.

> And so much more. All there in the local rag.
> All there, should I forget
> man isn't civilised quite, not yet.

Dolly Parton is five days older than me

Hot dang, we could be twins –

(Apart from
her moonshine spirit
her knock 'em dead talent
her dry as dust wit
her mountain of money
her tumbleweed hair
her backwoods backstory
and, outstandingly, her front)

we are sooooo alike, Dolly and me.
We even share the same star sign.

So why aren't I reading this at Glastonbury?

At Circular Quay

A ship as big as a small town,
(nine levels over the water),
docks in Sydney Harbour in a storm of flags and noise
and 6,290 American tourists disembark.

They amble to the quayside,
expressionless behind their shades,
supporting one another like
survivors from some catastrophe;
past the fish cafe and the tourist shop,
past Captain Cook's Harbour Tours ticket office
and the man pretending to be a statue.

They are drawn towards the haunting sound
coming from a man in a loin cloth,
painted like an Aborigine,
who squats on a blanket, blows on a didgeridoo,

as if he is calling them over vast distances
to some corroboree in the outback.
As if he has something important to tell them,
but has forgotten what it is.

For now, though, he wonders,
perhaps they would like to buy
a miniature boomerang?

A-Z of things not to do in the street

Please don't

Adulterate a Banksie,
engage in Chugging, Dealing,
Eating, Fighting, Grafittiing
(unless you *are* Banksie)

or any kind of Hanky-panky.
Irishdancing, Jaywalking,
Kerbcrawling, LitterLouting,
Mugging, Numbercrunching,
Ogling, Poetryreading, Quarrelling,
or Robbing banks.

Soliciting (see line six above),
Treading on the cracks,
Urinating, Vomiting, Whoring
(see lines six and fourteen above),
Xcessive Xercising, Yodelling,
inappropriateZipperopening
are not allowed.

Instead,

Buy an A - Z. Go home or get a room.
Do it there, if you must,
whatever it is you must do.
Just not in the street.

Thanks.

Street theatre

Two men, alike in awfulness,
disport themselves, hard by the library
where I pretend to work.

Enter a bawd, stage left.
It's clear they are familiars.
She leans upon a bollard,
stands, then falls.
They laugh. All laugh. They share her drink.

I'm trapped by books, but it's
these characters I read, as they perform
the shortened version of
the works of Shakespeare
(give or take a play)
for me, their unseen audience of one,
caught between spying and shelving,
life and art.

She tries on
the role of star-crossed lover.
They fight for her affections: she is
Doll Tearsheet, Portia, then a witch, a shrew.

I date-stamp a book,
turn back, and see a king dethroned,
a friend betrayed, a woman won:
then suddenly, all three cry havoc,
and it's over, finis; exit right,
pursued by a community policeman.

The running of the bulls

Thrice benediction:
the old priest, chanting the old words;
San Fermin…guide us in the bull run,
give us your blessing…
The vast crowd roars *Amen!*
Hanging from walls, from balconies,
behind flimsy barricades,
they taunt the runners, penned behind *policia*
– one great muscle straining to run, run
then noon, high noon, and the rocket sounds –
Corriendo!

Behind them the bulls, a galloping wall of meat
eyes rolling in fear   heads down   horns down
twelve at a time   barrelling out of Calle Santo Domingo –
and on through the narrow street that leads to
certain death
terrified men running before them
wishing they hadn't, wishing they were elsewhere;
in white shirts and red   for a five-minute frenzy
which ends in a scream when horns connect with flesh
and the bulls smell blood

                        and a young man
flies through the air and falls
while the crowd and the bulls roar over him
the boiling river of flesh won't, can't stop for him
his white face and the red blood on the white shirt
men on bulls   bulls on men   bellowing screaming
five men down and three men dead –

      In the arena, the bulls stand quietly now.
      Accepting, exhausted, heads down,
      until the last smoking breath of the last bull,
      all of them dead by sunset.

MH17

The man sleeps,
awkward in the cramped space.
His child wakes and whimpers,
reaches for his hand.

An announcement comes, ding ding,
the reassuring voice
talking of turbulence and seat belts.

And he wakes, too –
the last moment of innocence.

In that moment, through the window,
does he see the dreadful instrument
cut through the clouds
as fatefully as Harold's arrow,
too swift and sure for thoughts to form?

Only his instincts serve him now
as he grips his child's hand,
his body bending over, like a shield.

Full circle

Oh, we have a night life too, we old girls.
The small hours find us
wide awake and staggering, just like you,
drugged to the eyeballs high.
And in the morning we wake up
in someone else's trousers, just like you,
in someone else's bed;
not knowing how we got there
or how we are going to get home.

Aftermouth

Put yourself on auto-answer
lips moving to a preset tape.
You are no longer in charge
of tears, words.

For the duration, feeling is all you are.
You're public property,
watched and weighed.

Inabetterplace, one said.
You translate, can't believe your ears.
Words are disinterred
and rolled round the tongue,
then offered reverently, like wreaths.
Condolences. Eulogy.

I never saw her cry, another said
about a soul in torment.
Failing the tears test
is something you can't contemplate.

Cover your face.
Splutter the words ...*so kind,*
as tears fall down. They're satisfied.

Mouth the Lord's prayer, backwards.

The baby gardener

For her, it's four babies a day, twenty-five years of it,
all of them lost to her memory now,
except the first, burnt into her heart.

Stocky, with her grey crop and gardener's hands,
lifting young like new spuds out of the warm ground,
wiping them clean, with hands stubby and rough.

Her voice, harsh as a corncrake, tough as Gorbals,
yells *shout if you want, go on, push push push.*
She grabs, she probes, her hands on delicate places

made for a lover's touch.
She hands you over like a treasure found,
and vanishes. She has already forgotten you.

I take my mind off the things I am
and think of the things you will be.
Other now, the grown woman folded inside you
as the tree lies within the nut.

A teenage girl discusses the situation with her mother

Mother, she says. You always. You never.
Why did you? Whatever!
You shouldn't have bought it. I knew it. I swear it.
You wouldn't, don't actually tell me you couldn't –
you might have, you could have
if only you'd thought to. It's your fault.
Can't change it, I simply can't bear it,
just can't believe it – you won't let me wear it!

All other mothers are nicer by far.
I might have been, could have been,
would have been, should have been.
Now you inform me without any warning –
I'll never forgive you, I'll never forget it
why can't I stay out till Saturday morning?
You've ruined my life and you'll live to regret it,
what kind of a mother d'you think you are?

The old order

I don't remember how
the conversation got round to God
but suddenly my father
was strumphing at the end of the table,
everyone else zip-lipped.

It was like the time I snorted
when he said the sun never set
on the British Empire.
He stood up. I beat a hasty retreat,
my handkerchief a white flag.

When his arguments fell on deaf ears
he often raised his hand if not his game.
But anyway, I see it now,
now he's gone,
and the Empire's gone, and God, even God –

what it must have been like for him,
raised in that fortress of certainties,
to see it breached by his own daughter,
dammit, his *daughter*,
telling him what was what.

Grade Two Listed

Twenty-six births and seven deaths later,
the house has been Grade Two Listed.

Marriages have been celebrated here,
and divorces endured,
sometimes the other way round.

More than 100 backsides have perched
on that lavatory seat.
The lavatory has not been listed,
but will be preserved for ironic reasons.

The sash windows were painted shut in 1938.
During the war, every window was broken.
The coal hole opened its mouth
to its last load of nutty slack in 1975
(the coal hole lid is also Grade Two Listed).

The walls have buckled beneath the weight
of 36 coats of paint. Now everywhere is Farrow & Ball
(including the front door, which was previously painted
green, black, red white and blue).

The garden has been laid to lawn, dug for victory,
hedged about with box.
It acquired a shed and lost a shed,
embraced a conservatory and a greenhouse.
A pond was gouged out and filled in, gouged out
    and filled in.
Now a television aerial trembles on the chimney,
waiting for technology to render it redundant.

The windows have posted allegiance
to Whigs, Tories, Labour and Liberals,
but not, so far, UKIP. The house itself is neutral.

Something very bad happened here in 1931,
but the house is not telling.
Nothing like it will ever happen again,
now it has been Grade Two Listed.

Tomorrow I will pull myself together

From the sludge of the fifty-sixth morning, I wake –
reach out to the cold His-Side-of-the-Bed
and shout to the world *oh sod it – can't bear it –*
and, unwashed, crawl to my favourite chair,
where his portrait hangs on the living room wall,
(oh, the irony) young again, happy and well.

Soon comes the first of many debates
between me and that painted face up there.
Tell me the truth darling once and for all –
Where are you? How could you
desert us like that, without any warning?
I fill in the answers he'd never have said.

I'd love to fall into the painting, like Alice,
or Orpheus, roaming through heaven or hell
to find him again. The one bloody soul mate
I'm likely to meet, is dead (yes, I know it)
yet still seems so *vastly* alive, looking down
from his place on the wall, in a singular way
that's loving one minute and angry the next,
at me in pyjamas, with him in my head.

It's late afternoon when the vicar comes calling,
although I have long since abandoned belief
and she says *My dear girl,*
let go of your grief. Don't cry any longer;
come here, let me hug you –
he's gone home to God, to a much better place,
he waits for you there (I know it, I feel it)
he wouldn't have wanted to linger in pain.

She gathers me into her dusty embrace
and I think, Oh, he would have,
if only he could have. He'd rather be here,
than bloody well dead –
and I glance at his painted shade on the wall
and fancy he winks at me, over her head.

I did it for you

The knife in the back, the cruel remark,
the pilfering, threatening, just for a lark,

my hand in your purse, my hand in the till,
the fiddle and faddle with Grandmother's will,

the little white lie, the hideous laugh,
the leisurely walk down the primrose path,

the hand in your blouse, the grope in the park,
the sexual assault that was 'only a lark',

the sordid affair, deserting my kids
and leaving my wife with her life on the skids,

the knife in your neck, the bomb on the bus,
the bomb on the train, I did it for us!

I'd do it again! I'd do it today,
I did it for you. What more can I say?

Acknowledgments

'To the front as night is falling' won first prize in the Grey Hen Poetry Competition, 2013. 'Watching my mother turn into a wasp' won third prize in the Second Light Poetry Competition, 2014.

Other poems have appeared in anthologies, including *The Book of Love and Loss* (2014), *Fanfare* (2015), *The Forward Prize Anthology* (pick of 20 years), *Running Before the Wind* (Grey Hen Press) and *Shades of Meaning* (Grey Hen Press); and in poetry magazines such as *Magma*, *The Frogmore Papers*, and *ARTEMIS*; *Ink, Sweat and Tears* (online), *Interpreter's House*, *Acumen* and *Mslexia*.